CLANG, BOOM, BANG

Library of Congress Cataloging-in-Publication Data
Moncure, Jane Belk.
Clang, boom, bang / Jane Belk-Moncure;
illustrated by Viki Woodworth.
p. cm.
Summary: Simple rhymes describe a variety of
sounds, from the exuberant noises of a circus parade to the
many different sounds heard in nature.
ISBN 1-56766-285-4 (smythe-sewn library bound)

[1. Sound — Fiction. 2. Stories in rhyme.] I. Title.
PZ0.3.M72C1 1997   97-6269
[E] — dc21   CIP
                                                         AC

BY JANE BELK-MONCURE / ILLUSTRATED BY VIKI WOODWORTH

CLANG, BOOM, BANG

THE CHILD'S WORLD

I hear loud crowd sounds up and down the street.

"Tap, tap tap," go marching feet.

With a clang, boom, bang,
"Hip, hip, hurray!"

The circus parade is in town today.

I hear "rat-a-tat-tats"
and "tum-a-tum-tums."

Toots and whistles,
horns and drums.

Elephants march.
Balloons go "pop."

Circus ponies go
"clippity-clop."
Loud crowd sounds
are all around.

I hear fun-time sounds in the city park:
balls and bats and roller-skate wheels,
jump rope, hopscotch,
giggles and squeals.

"Bump" goes
the see-saw.
"Swish" goes
the swing.

Bells on the
merry-go-round
ding-a-ling.

I hear country sounds when I go to the farm. I hear "moos" and "baas" and a "cockle-doodle-do."

I hear "oinks" and "quacks" and "gobbles," too.

Some sounds are high
like jingle bells ringing.

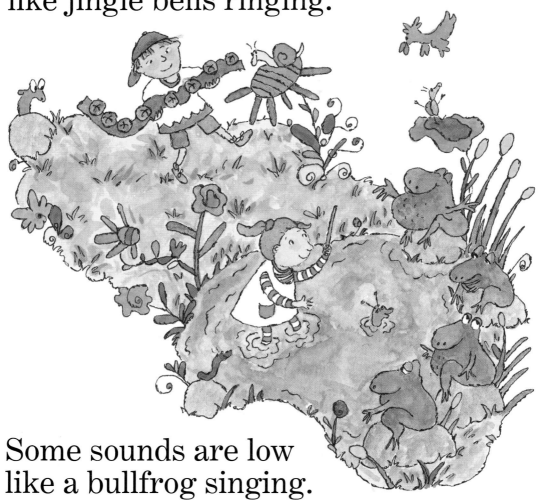

Some sounds are low
like a bullfrog singing.

Some sounds are fast like popcorn popping, "pop, pop, pop."

Some sounds are slow like raindrops dropping, "drip, drip, drop."

A sound may be as soft as a whisper
in your ear when I tell you a secret
no one else can hear.

A sound may be a tiptoe when my sister takes a nap, curled up like a kitten in my Mommy's lap.

A sound may be a sad "Good-bye"
when someone goes away.

A sound may be a happy "Hi" when someone comes to play.

I hear sounds in the morning when
I open the window wide.

I hear "chirps" and tiny "peeps" and a flutter of wings outside.

My ears are like a telephone I wear on my head.

My ears stay busy all day long, and when I go to bed my ears are sleepy.

They hear me say "Good night"
and "I love you."

When I go to sleep at night
I think my ears do too.